So Yummy brings you another easy-to-follow, step-by-step cookbook jam-packed with hacks, tips and ideas for your next dinner party. Whether it's with your friends, family or even your cat, this book will level-up your food presentation and hosting skills. Not only will it look like you have it all together but you'll learn to be a wiz in the kitchen too!

Each section is packed with gorgeous yet simple plating tips and recipes you can't wait to show off. From churro tacos to edible birthday candles and chocolate ice cream bowls, this book will show you how to create your own dishes and pair them perfectly.

This book is not only your secret weapon, but it contains links to exclusive content with recipes and pairing ideas that are only accessible through So Yummy! You'll get tips like, how to throw the perfect taco party, how-to-videos for cake decorating techniques as well as food styling pro-tips to make your food look Instagram-ready!

Love to entertain? You'll find, plating techniques, chocolate sculpture hacks and one of a kind recipes written by our So Yummy experts just for you! Basically, This book has everything! Enough with the reading… Let's get cooking!

PICTURE PERFECT COOKING

Gorgeous recipes you'll want to snap, tag and share!

Dedicated to our fans who crave beautiful and bright food that tastes just as good as it looks!

TABLE OF CONTENTS

06 Kitchen Essentials

08 Spellbinding Chocolate Spinout

12 Chocolate Water Art

16 Chocolate Iceberg Ahead!

20 Chocolate Brush Cakes

24 Edible Spin Art

28 Splatter Fruit Tart

32 Chocolate Monogram Stamps

36 Sugary Sweet Sunrise

40 Fancy Fruit Smash

44 Strawberry Ring of Fire

48 My Sweet Valentine

CHURRO CHOCO TACOS PG. 78

3-LAYERED STRAWBERRY FIELD CAKE PG. 104

SUSHI PLATING PG. 23

This cookbook is your key to becoming the ultimate picture-perfect dinner party host.

CRISPY BLUEBERRY CROISSANTS PG. 68

52 Berry Blossom Tart

56 Caramel Bubble Bark

60 Caged in Caramel

64 Spin Me Some Sugar

68 Crispy Blueberry Croissants

72 Galaxy Vegan Cheesecakes

78 Churro Choco Tacos

84 Upgrade Your Toast Game

88 Incredible Edible Balloons

92 Wedding Cake Goals

96 Edible Birthday Candles

100 Chocolate Lace Cage Cake

104 3-Layered Strawberry Field Cake

108 Purple Ombré Cake

112 Checkerboard Neapolitan Cake

116 Magical Monet Cake

WHAT TO LOOK FOR ON OUR PAGES

FUN FACT

Origin stories and other juicy info about your favorite dishes and ingredients.

MAKE IT VEGAN

Suggestions for vegan-friendly swaps!

EXCLUSIVE CONTENT

Brand-new expert tutorials and So Yummy recipes you won't find anywhere else!

 Watch the recipe video

+ freezing time
10
1 SPIRAL

SPELLBINDING CHOCOLATE SPINOUT

You are under my spell...Give me all of your chocolate! Hypnotize your guests with this **impressive chocolate spiral**!

INGREDIENTS:

Tempered dark chocolate

Piping bag with fine tip

> A gentle touch and a few key tools are all you need to perfect this chocolate spiral. Be sure to create your spiral on parchment paper for easy peel and transfer using a large palette knife (spatula works too!) to keep the spiral flat. Then, simply "slinky" it over the dessert with care.
>
> — Rachel

STEP 1

STEP 2

STEP 3

DIRECTIONS:

1. Create a spiral by piping chocolate onto a lazy Susan while spinning it clockwise.

2. After the chocolate is set, but pliable, lift the chocolate off of the plate from the center.

3. Place the spiral on top of a brownie sundae and serve.

EXCLUSIVE CONTENT!

ARE YOU CUCKOO FOR COCOA?!

Watch for more ways to drench your life in chocolate!

Watch the recipe video

1 SPIRAL

CHOCOLATE WATER ART

You must be a modern day Michael Angelo because this **chocolate work of art** looks like it should be in a museum.

INGREDIENTS:

Tempered chocolate in a piping bag with a fine tip

2 cups ice water in a round glass

Have your melted chocolate at a lukewarm temperature before you drizzle it into the water, then, once it's formed its sculpture shape, you want to be very gentle pulling it out - it's a delicate little work of art.

— *Dorie*

13

STEP 1

STEP 2

STEP 3

STEP 4

DIRECTIONS:

1. Quickly drizzle tempered chocolate into a cup of ice water in a circular motion.

2. Allow chocolate to set for a minute or two until firm.

3. Carefully remove the chocolate sculpture from the water using tweezers.

4. Place your masterpiece on top of a few scoops of sorbet or ice cream with whipped cream.

MAKE WILLY
WONKA JEALOUS

Watch this video to get more chocolate covered inspiration!

Watch the recipe video

1 BOWL

CHOCOLATE ICEBERG AHEAD!

You don't have to visit the glaciers to enjoy this **chocolate concoction**, because this iceberg ice cream bowl will have you doing the splits!

INGREDIENTS:

Tempered dark chocolate

Ice cubes

"

These chocolate icebergs are like mini sculptures and not one will ever be the same as the last. Before trying to pry the chocolate from the ice, be sure to let the ice melt a little bit, so that it naturally pulls away from the chocolate. Then, use all the little nooks and crannies as individual serving pedestals, perfect for whipped cream, mini ice cream scoops and fruits.

— Tess

STEP 1

STEP 2

STEP 3

STEP 4

STEP 5

DIRECTIONS:

1. Place about 2 cups of ice on a plate or shallow bowl.
2. Pour about ¼ cup tempered chocolate over the ice cubes.
3. Allow to set for about **5 minutes** until firm.
4. Flip the chocolate upside down to reveal an artistic bowl!
5. Fill with mint chip ice cream, whipped cream, ice cream sandwich pieces and a cherry on top!

Oh Snap That Looks Good!

It might look pretty in person, but try these techniques to make your culinary creation jump off your feed!

DIRECTIONS:

1. Always use natural light. Take the plate outside into the shade or choose a seat near the window at your favorite eatery.

2. Take the photo from overhead. Overhead photos capture the color, shape and texture of the dish or tablescape in a way that no other angle can.

3. Try to find interesting backgrounds. Sometimes a scrap of paper or an old brick wall can make the photo more interesting.

4. Shoot food that you love to eat! Stay in your own lane and stick to the subjects you are passionate about. It comes across in the photo.

5. Use the light from your friend's phone. Light + more light = a trending photo.

6. Download a photo app. After you've snapped your picture, take the time to enhance it using one of several great photo editing apps!

Watch the recipe video

SERVES 1

CHOCOLATE BRUSH CAKES

Maybe I should start replacing my bronzer with chocolate because this dessert technique is a **stroke of cocoa genius**!

INGREDIENTS:

Chocolate fudge

Squeeze bottle

Clean 2 inch paint brush

Store-bought mini chocolate desserts

"

When using a squeeze bottle, test your design on a paper towel first to get comfortable with the lines.

– *Dorie*

STEP 1

STEP 2

STEP 3

DIRECTIONS:

1. Create 3 staggered lines of fudge on a white plate using a piping bag or squeeze bottle.

2. Next, using a clean pastry brush, brush the lines in an upward motion to create chocolate brush strokes.

3. Place a store-bought mini chocolate cake, cheesecake and macaron at the base of each brush stroke.

SUSHI PLATING TECHNIQUE

A paint brush isn't the only way to deck out your dinner party! You'll never guess what tool we used to serve up this sushi supper!

SERVES 1

EDIBLE SPIN ART

You might need to reserve a spot for this edible spin class because everyone's going to want to **get in on it**!

INGREDIENTS:

Strawberry fruit puree

Raspberry fruit puree

Store-bought macarons

STEP 1

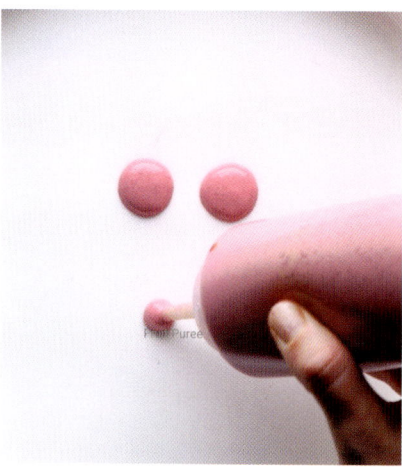

STEP 2

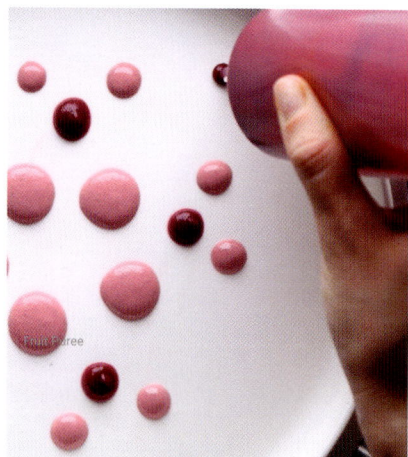

STEP 3

STEP 4

DIRECTIONS:

1. Place 5 large drops of strawberry puree in the center of a white round plate.

2. Place smaller drops of raspberry puree in between the strawberry and repeat until the plate is covered.

3. Place the plate onto a lazy susan and spin to give your plate a "spin art" effect.

4. Place 3 macarons in the middle of your artistic creation and serve!

YOU ARE WHAT YOU DRINK

Find your sign and see what your next order should be based on your zodiac sign.

Airy Aries Cocktail

ARIES
MARCH 21 — APRIL 19

Bubbly, daring and brave. Aries, you appreciate the sweet things in life. This perfect combo of sweet sorbet and bubbly rose is the perfect way to perk up the party just like you!

Taurus Margarita Bomb

TAURUS
APRIL 20 — MAY 20

Transparent, stubborn, luxurious. This margarita is so over the top with it's unique smokey ice sphere. Taurus loves to make a statement and this cocktail is no exception.

Gemini Gin and Tonic

GEMINI
MAY 21 — JUNE 20

Lively, expressive and adaptable. This unique spin on gin and tonic is familiar yet complicated, which embodies the Gemini spirit perfectly.

Cancer Mood Ring Shots

CANCER
JUNE 21 — JULY 22

Moody, imaginative and caring. These colorful shots that are flavored with blue curacao, grenadines and vodka are sure to please your palate no matter what your current mood might be!

Leo Flaming Sunset

LEO
JULY 23 — AUGUST 22

Elegant, courageous and entertaining. If a cocktail had a personality, this one would definitely be an extrovert. Leo, you stand out from the crowd and that's why a sweet and fiery cocktail is the perfect match.

Virgo Cuervo

VIRGO
AUGUST 23 — SEPTEMBER 22

Precise, resourceful and clean. Virgo, you don't like to waste time with anything frivolous. You like to avoid drama at all costs. The clean cucumber, seltzer and tequila in this cocktail allows you to appreciate the simple things in life.

Libra Colada

LIBRA
SEPTEMBER 23 — OCTOBER 22

Hospitable, balanced and charming. The epitome of balance is a cocktail blended with whole fruit and a dash of rum. You like to play, but you always have your head on straight.

Scorpio Bourbon Squeeze

SCORPIO
OCTOBER 23 — NOVEMBER 21

Ambitious, dramatic and strong. This mysterious martini is made with just bourbon and blood orange with a smokey spritz of orange oil to finish. You never hold back and always hold your ground which is why Scorpios always make great partners. They'll always have your back.

Smokey Sagittarius

SAGITTARIUS
NOVEMBER 22 — DECEMBER 21

Wise, dedicated and old fashioned. Smoked rosemary, bitters and bourbon represent your in depth and complex personality.

Capricorn Sagetini

CAPRICORN
DECEMBER 22 — JANUARY 19

Ambitious, clever and confident. This martini is just like you Capricorn. Made with pineapple, vodka, sage and egg white to make it extra frothy, this drink really stands out from the crowd.

Fizzy Aquarius

AQUARIUS
JANUARY 20 — FEBRUARY 18

Quirky, Clever and aloof. This fruity and refreshing cocktail is the perfect pick me up for the always bubbly and friendly Aquarius.

Pisces Fish Bowl

PISCES
FEBRUARY 19 — MARCH 20

Sweet, dreamy and fantastic. You are just the sweetest and so is this fantastic pitcher filled with coconut rum, blue curacao and sprite.

 Watch the recipe video

SERVES 1

SPLATTER FRUIT TART

Did Picasso make this dessert? Oh wait...you did! Some call it a mess, but we call it **delicious**!

INGREDIENTS:

Mango fruit puree

Raspberry fruit puree

Carrot or cantaloupe puree

> Anytime you plate a sauce component, whether it's a splatter, a splish or a swish, it's all about confidence. If you're hesitant or cautious, the result will reflect that. The key is to be loose in the wrist and casual about it. If you're making a splatter - go for it and just give it a whack! The more you try to control the end result, the less impressive it will be.
>
> —Tess

STEP 1　　　　　　**STEP 2**　　　　　　**STEP 3**

STEP 4　　　　　　**STEP 5**

DIRECTIONS:

1. In the center of a small round dessert plate, use a squeeze bottle filled with yellow fruit puree such as mango to create a quarter sized circle in the center of a large white plate.

2. Next place a nickel sized circle of an orange red fruit puree such as carrot or cantaloupe into the center of the yellow dot.

3. Finally place a dime sized circle of a red puree such as raspberry into the center of the orange circle.

4. Use a spoon to "smack" the center of the circle to create a colorful splatter effect.

5. Top the fruity art piece with a miniature fruit tartlet.

REFRESHING ROSÉ SANGRIA

Now you can tell your friends you are having fruit salad for dinner! Well, fruit salad soaked in wine, but that's irrelevant at this point.

1 Add the fruit and sugar to a large bowl and stir.

1 cup sliced strawberries

1 cup raspberries

1 cup sliced peaches

2 tablespoons granulated cane sugar

¼ cup Triple Sec

2 Add the Triple Sec to the fruit and allow to soak for 20 minutes to 1 hour.

3 Place the ice in a large pitcher and top with the fruit mixture.

2 cups ice

1 750ml bottle sparkling rosé

4 Pour in the bottle of rosé and sparkling water.

2 cups sparkling water

5 Garnish with mint and serve in sugar rimmed glasses.

10 mint leaves for garnish

Watch the recipe video

12 STAMPS

CHOCOLATE MONOGRAM STAMPS

Get ready to Instagram these mini monograms! Invite your guests to your next party with **adorable chocolate stamps** because let's face it, wax just doesn't taste as good.

INGREDIENTS:

Tempered dark, milk and white chocolate

Ice cold wax seal stamp

Piping bag fitted with a small round tip

> Melt your chocolate gently and check it often; as soon as it's soft enough to stir to smoothness, cut the heat to avoid it seizing up permanently.
>
> – Dorie

33

STEP 1

STEP 2

STEP 3

DIRECTIONS:

1. Pipe quarter sized circles of dark, milk, and white chocolate onto a piece or waxed paper or parchment.

2. Using the chilled stamp to carefully imprint each circle. Keep chilling the stamp if necessary.

3. Place the stamped discs on mini cupcakes for a personalized touch!

IT'S ALL IN THE SIGNS!

Use our chocolate zodiac chart to guide you on your path to find cocoa bliss.

Chocolate Easter Bunny

ARIES
MARCH 21 – APRIL 19

Adventurous Aries has a daring and childlike spirit that make nostalgic kid-friendly foods their go-to when it comes to cravings! Chicken tenders, french fries and holiday chocolates always hit the spot after a long day of conquests.

Dark Chocolate Truffles

TAURUS
APRIL 20 – MAY 20

Because Taurus is an earth sign ruled by Venus, you tend to like the finer things in life. You LOVE your food and when you indulge it must be worth it.

Chocolate Covered Pretzels

GEMINI
MAY 21 – JUNE 20

Gemini, because you are an air sign that is symbolized by twins, your mood can change on a whim. Some days you want a sweet treat and the next something salty! Chocolate covered pretzels are the perfect mix of sweet, salty and crunchy and is sure to satisfy both sides of your personality.

Choco Flan

CANCER
JUNE 21 – JULY 22

Because cancer is a sensitive water sign, you tend to learn toward anything creamy, comforting and decadent. Choco flan delivers a rich and creamy flan texture along with a deep cocoa flavored cake. It's a dessert you want to wrap yourself up in!

A Chocolate Fountain

LEO
JULY 23 – AUGUST 22

Leo, you are a theatrical, glamorous and over the top performer who loves to the be the center of attention. You love drenching all of your favorite foods in a blanket of chocolate.

Almond Butter Truffles

VIRGO
AUGUST 23 – SEPTEMBER 22

Almond butter truffles- Because you are sensual, earth conscious, slightly uptight sign of well-being, the almond butter truffle is the perfect balance of good and evil. It's creamy, salty and sweet all at once and you don't feel too neurotic after eating one.

Chocolate Bark

LIBRA
SEPTEMBER 23 – OCTOBER 22

Because you are the sign of balance, you like to top your chocolate bark with nuts, dried fruit and a drizzle of white chocolate. After all, isn't balance what life's all about?

Mexican Chocolate

SCORPIO
OCTOBER 23 – NOVEMBER 21

A delicate dance between sweet and spicy perfectly represents Scorpio's intensity and mysterious attributes. What begins as a sweet bite, quickly turns into a spicy surprise that not everyone was expecting.

Double Chocolate Cheesecake

SAGITTARIUS
NOVEMBER 22 – DECEMBER 21

Because Sagittarius is the mythic god of the feast, your sign lives life in excess. You love indulging in over the top and ridiculously sweet desserts that only the true chocolate lover can appreciate.

Chocolate Chip Cookie

CAPRICORN
DECEMBER 22 – JANUARY 19

Capricorn is a traditional earth sign who likes order and tradition. The simple chocolate chip cookie is a comforting and consistent dessert that never fails to impress.

Peppermint Hot Chocolate

AQUARIUS
JANUARY 20 – FEBRUARY 18

Aquarius is the zodiac's most friendly sign. The best way to warm up and still keep that pep in your step during the cold winter seasons is with a warm mug filled with minty hot chocolate. You like to keep things interesting, which is why everyone loves you!

Chocolate Crepe Cake

PISCES
FEBRUARY 19- MARCH 20

Chocolate crepe cake- Because Pisces is said to embody all of the traits of the zodiac, a chocolate crepe cake, which has many layers is the perfect representation of never ending deliciousness!

Watch the recipe video

SUGARY SWEET SUNRISE

Good Morning Sunshine! You'll never guess what tool you need to make this powdered sugar sunrise!

INGREDIENTS:

Powdered sugar

Swiss roll slice

Paper Towel

Apple cutter

> To keep your sugar from clumping, store it in a sealed glass container with a teaspoon of uncooked white rice at the bottom to absorb moisture.
>
> — Mike

SERVES 1

STEP 1

STEP 2

STEP 3

STEP 4

STEP 5

DIRECTIONS:

1. Place paper towel over ½ of a dark plate of piece of slate.

2. Center an apple cutter on the plate overlapping the paper towel.

3. Sprinkle powdered sugar over the plate.

4. Remove apple cutter and paper towel.

5. Place a swiss roll slice on the opposite side of the powdered sugar pattern. Decorate the plate with fresh raspberries.

FUN FACT

A Swiss roll, jelly roll, roll cake, or cream roll is a type of sponge cake roll filled with whipped cream, jam, or icing. The origins of the term are unclear. In spite of the name "Swiss roll", the cake is believed to have originated elsewhere in Central Europe, likely Austria.

Watch the recipe video

40

SERVES 1

FANCY FRUIT SMASH

Put on those fancy pants because you'll be doing a disco dance with this **perfectly pretty** plating!

INGREDIENTS:

Raspberry puree

Store-bought mini chocolate cake

Squeeze bottle

Measuring cup with flat bottom

> "
> You can experiment with different shaped/textured lids and varying amounts of pressure to create unique squish patterns. The only limit is your imagination (and what's in your kitchen drawer)
>
> – Mike

STEP 1

STEP 2

STEP 3

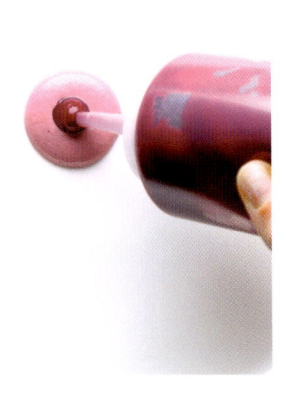

STEP 4

DIRECTIONS:

1. Place a quarter sized dollop of raspberry puree in the center of a white using a squeeze bottle.

2. Use a flat bottomed measuring cup or glass to press down evenly in the center.

3. Lift up the measuring cup to reveal a design that looks good enough to eat!

4. Place a small chocolate cake just to the side of the fruit puree and garnish with edible flowers.

> **Eating is a necessity, but cooking is an art.**

— **Gasine Lemcke**

Watch the recipe video

SERVES 1

STRAWBERRY RING OF FIRE

Find someone who **loves dessert** as much as you do! If you're lucky, maybe you'll put a ring on it!

INGREDIENTS:

Raspberry jam

Freeze dried raspberries

Mini strawberry cheesecake

> If you're looking for a different thickness in your ring, try adding apple juice to thin out your preserves, a little bit at a time, until you get your desired consistency!
>
> – Mike

STEP 1

STEP 2

STEP 3

STEP 4

DIRECTIONS:

1. Dip the rim of a small glass bowl into raspberry jam.
2. Stamp the bowl in the center of a large white plate.
3. Sprinkle freeze dried raspberries over the entire plate.
4. Remove the glass bowl and place a small strawberry cheesecake in the center of the circle.

ABOVE AND BEYOND

Check out more super fancy ways to impress the pants off your guests! Unless it's your parents... That's just awkward.

Watch the recipe video

48

SERVES 1

MY SWEET VALENTINE

Make cupid proud with this adorable dessert that will have your **sweetie seeing hearts**!

INGREDIENTS:

Melted white chocolate

Strawberry fruit puree

Store-bought mini cupcake

STEP 1

STEP 2

STEP 3

STEP 4

DIRECTIONS:

1. Place a large circle of melted white chocolate on a round dessert plate. Using a squeeze bottle filled with strawberry fruit puree.

2. Place a spiral of pink dots inside the larger white circle.

3. Drag a wooden skewer through the dots in a circular motion to create a chain of miniature hearts!

4. Place your cupcake in the center and prepare to fall in love!

TIME FOR A COFFEE BREAK

Taking the time to make the perfect espresso drink can be the highlight of your day. Here is a guide to making craveable cafe-worthy beverages.

ESPRESSO
1 shot espresso

LATTE
⅔ espresso + ⅓ steamed milk

CAPPUCCINO
⅓ espresso + ⅓ hot milk + ⅓ foam

AMERICANO
⅓ espresso + ⅔ water

FLAT WHITE
⅓ espresso + ⅔ steamed milk

MACCHIATO
double shot espresso + steamed milk

BREVE
⅓ espresso + ⅔ half & half

MOCHA
⅗ espresso + ⅕ chocolate + ⅕ steamed milk

AFFOGATO
2 shots espresso + 1 scoop vanilla ice cream

Watch the recipe video

5

SERVES 1

BERRY BLOSSOM TART

Take a moment to stop and smell the roses! Your **culinary skills will blossom** after trying this fanciful dessert plating!

INGREDIENTS:

Raspberry puree

Small berry tart

Squeeze bottle

> If your puree is too runny, heat it up on the stove top, then separately mix 1 tablespoon cornstarch with 1 tablespoon of cold water; add the cornstarch slurry in small increments to the hot puree until it's thickened to your liking.
>
> — *Dorie*

STEP 1 **STEP 2** **STEP 3**

DIRECTIONS:

1. On a plain white plate draw 8 quarter sized circles using the raspberry puree to form a circle.

2. Using the backside of a teaspoon, drag the swirls to the center of a plate creating petal shapes.

3. Place a berry tart in the center of the flower.

EXCLUSIVE CONTENT

HOW TO MAKE ANYTHING PUREE

Care to play with more puree? Scan here to watch this exclusive video for more ideas on how to keep you next dish from "blending" in with the crowd!

Watch the recipe video

SERVES 1

CARAMEL BUBBLE BARK

Time to raid your grandparent's candy dish because this caramel cupcake topper is sure to **break you out of your bubble**!

INGREDIENTS:

1 Caramel hard candy

"

You can also bake the caramel candy to create the bubble effect! For both methods, pro tip, do not walk away or you will over cook the caramel.

— Tennille

STEP 1

STEP 2

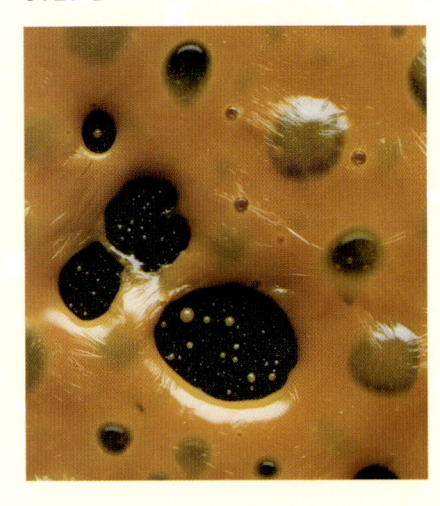

STEP 3

STEP 4

DIRECTIONS:

1. Place an unwrapped caramel hard candy in the center of a non-stick frying pan over medium heat.

2. Allow caramel to melt and bubble.

3. Let caramel cool completely in pan.

4. Using a spatula, remove the caramel and place it on top of a vanilla cupcake.

WHATS THE DIFFERENCE?

CARAMEL

vs

BUTTER SCOTCH

FUN FACT

Caramel is a mix of white granulated sugar, heavy whipping cream, butter, and a dash of vanilla, while butterscotch is made with brown sugar instead of white sugar and was known as just a hard candy.

Watch the recipe video

⏱ 5
SERVES 1

CAGED IN CARAMEL

Lock me up and throw away the key! I'm not sure if this **sugar cage** is secure enough to keep any dessert safe.

INGREDIENTS:

1 cup granulated sugar

1 tbsp water

"

Freeze and grease the metal spoon before drizzling the caramel and it will harden and come off easy!

– Tennille

STEP 1

STEP 2

STEP 3

STEP 4

STEP 5

STEP 6

DIRECTIONS:

1. Heat a non-stick skillet over medium heat. Add sugar and water and stir to combine. Stir constantly until sugar melts and becomes a golden caramel shade. Carefully drizzle the hot caramel over the back of a ladle.

2. Allow to cool, remove the caramel cage and repeat.

3. Place one cage in the center of a white plate.

4. Scoop 5 mini scoops of vanilla ice cream inside.

5. Sprinkle with cookie crumbs.

6. Top with brownie pieces and the second caramel cage and serve!

EXPLORE THE "PASTA-BILITIES"

Serve this restaurant quality dessert with your favorite pasta dish! Make sure to check out this carb filled chart to double check you are doing your pasta sauce justice!

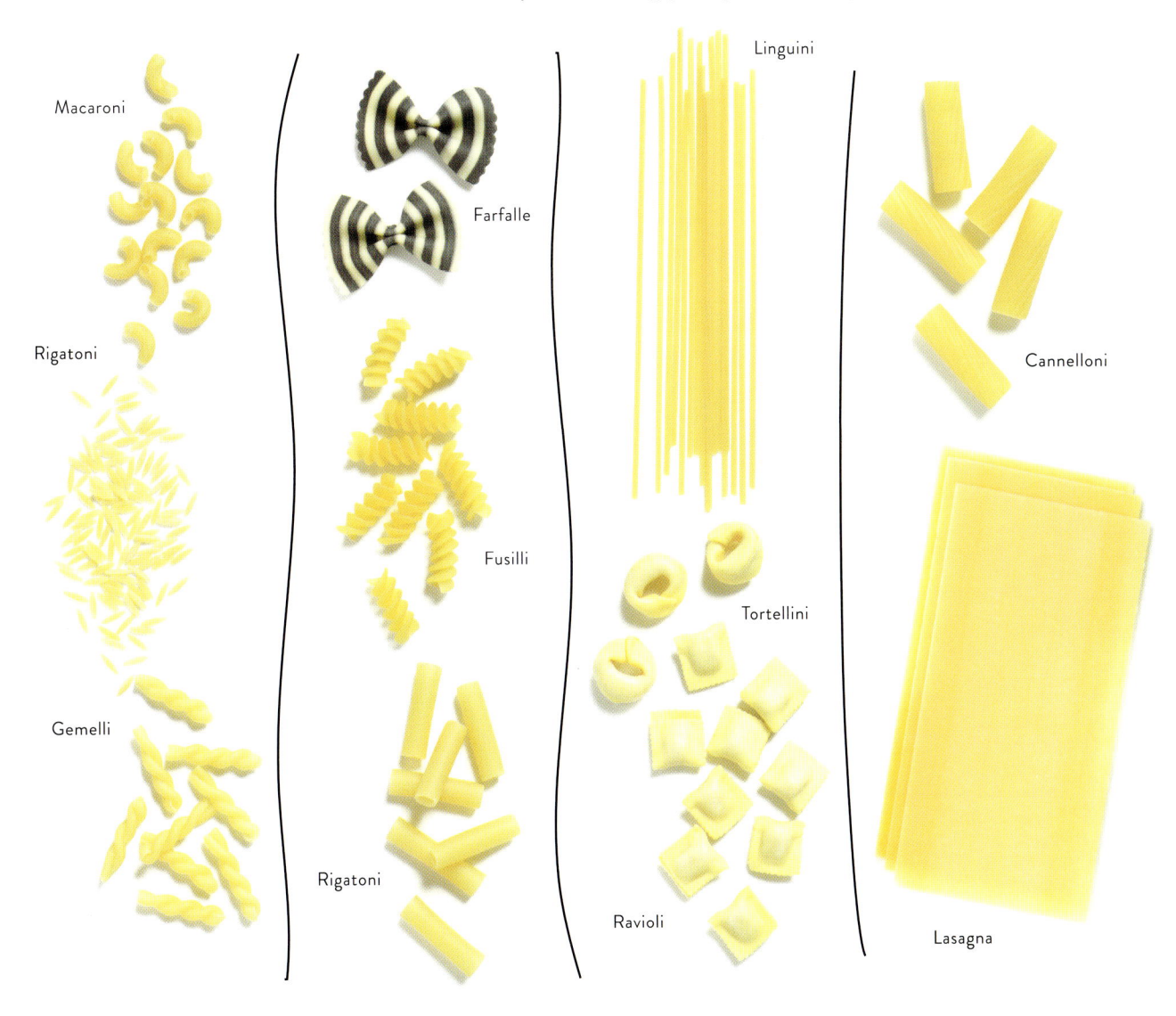

Macaroni

Rigatoni

Gemelli

Farfalle

Fusilli

Rigatoni

Linguini

Tortellini

Ravioli

Cannelloni

Lasagna

These pasta shapes might be mini, but they add big texture to soups, sides and salads. You can add them to any dish!

These fun-sized pasta shapes are round and have multiple ridges to hold light flakes of garlic, lemon zest or chunks of tomato.

The proof is in the pasta. This particular pasta doesn't need much to make them irresistible. Serve them with lighter sauces, they can easily become overpowered.

Extra large pasta shapes like these can handle thick cheese fillings like ricotta and meat and can withstand being baked in the oven at high temperatures without falling apart.

63

Watch the recipe video

SPIN ME SOME SUGAR

I'm not going to sugar coat it, when you serve this **nest**, your guests may not want to leave.

SERVES 2

INGREDIENTS:

1 cup granulated sugar

1 tbsp water

> Melted sugar is hot, hot, hot! Be very careful as you master this spun sugar. Practice makes perfect with this technique.
>
> — Dorie

STEP 1

STEP 2

STEP 3

STEP 4

STEP 5

DIRECTIONS:

1. Heat a non-stick skillet over medium heat. Add sugar and water and stir to combine. Stir constantly until sugar melts and becomes a golden caramel shade.

2. Use a metal slotted spoon to scoop up some of the hot caramel.

3. Drizzle the caramel over a hand mixer fitted with one beater on medium speed until a sugar nest forms.

4. Carefully remove the caramel nest from the beater.

5. Place the nest on top of an Oreo crust cheesecake.

SHHH DON'T TELL YOUR DENTIST!

Check out this exclusive content for more sugary expectations that are sure to satisfy your sweet tooth.

Watch the recipe video

+ cooling time
60
SERVES 8

CRISPY BLUEBERRY CROISSANTS

Hurry up and **butter up your besties** with these blueberry croissants...Or keep them all to yourself. That works too.

INGREDIENTS:

Croissant dough

½ cup blueberries

¼ cup lemon zest

2 tbsp powdered sugar

2 sticks unsalted butter, softened

FUN FACT

Croissants are actually Austrian. Yep. While the croissant may just be one of the most quintessentially French things you can find, it was actually invented in Austria. The croissant - or Kipferl as the Austrians call it - was filling people up from way back in the 13th century.

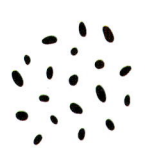

STEP 1

STEP 2

STEP 3

STEP 4

STEP 5

STEP 6

STEP 7

STEP 8

STEP 9

70

STEP 10

STEP 11

DIRECTIONS:

1. Using a hand mixer beat blueberries, lemon zest, powdered sugar, and ¼ cup lemon zest into the softened butter until fully incorporated.

2. Transfer butter to a parchment lined 8 x 8 pan and top with another piece of parchment paper.

3. Use a spatula to flatten the butter and freeze for **30 minutes** to overnight.

4. On a floured surface, roll the croissant dough into a large diamond shape.

5. Place the chilled blueberry butter in the center and fold in the corners like an envelope.

6. Press the rolling pin into the dough every few inches from top to bottom, this breaks up the butter square and incorporates it into the dough to give it it's signature flaky layers.

7. Roll the dough into a large disc then fold the dough into thirds. Turn the dough clockwise and repeat; break up the butter, roll, fold, turn.

8. After the third turn, wrap the dough in plastic wrap and refrigerate for a minimum of **two hours**.

9. Roll the chilled dough on a floured surface to about ⅛ inch thick.

10. Slice your dough into triangles. At the base of each triangle, place three or four blueberries, and then roll them into crescent shapes as tightly as you can.

11. Brush the rolled up croissants with egg white and bake at **400°F** for **35-40 minutes** until golden brown. Serve on a platter with candied lemons.

Watch the recipe video

VEGAN

SERVES 6

GALAXY VEGAN CHEESECAKES

These galaxy **vegan** cheesecakes are best eaten with the dark side of the spoon!

INGREDIENTS:

1 cup blackberries

1 cup blueberries

1 cup raspberries

3 cups raw cashews

1 cup coconut cream

¾ cup maple syrup

½ cup lemon juice

2 tsp vanilla

½ cup coconut oil

1 tbsp blue algae

1 cup raw almonds

10 dates, pitted

1 cup raw walnuts

¾ cup unsweetened shredded coconut

¼ tsp sea salt

STEP 1 STEP 2  STEP 3

STEP 4  STEP 5 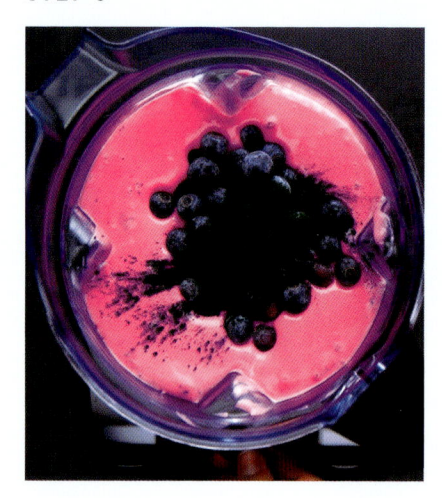 STEP 6

STEP 7  STEP 8  STEP 9

STEP 10

STEP 11

STEP 12

DIRECTIONS:

1. Freeze blackberries, blueberries and raspberries on a large plate until firm.

2. Blend cashews, coconut cream, maple syrup, lemon juice, vanilla and coconut oil in a high-speed blender for **4 minutes**.

3. Reserve ¼ of the mixture in a small bowl to use as the white cheesecake layer.

4. Add raspberries and blend. Set aside ¼ mixture.

5. Add blueberries and blue algae and blend. Set aside ¼ mixture.

6. Add blackberries and blend. Set aside.

7. In the bowl of a food processor fitted with the chopping blade, combine almonds, dates, walnuts, shredded coconut and sea salt for about **5 minutes** until the mixture is finely chopped and resembles wet sand.

8. Transfer mixture to a muffin tin lined with parchment paper using a ¼ cup measure and press down firmly.

9. Layer the pink, blue and purple mixtures on top of the crust and top with the white mixture.

10. Freeze cheesecakes for **30 minutes** to overnight.

11. Decorate the cheesecakes with any leftover filling using a piping bag.

12. Top with golden star shaped sprinkles.

75

BEGIN WITH
COSMIC CHEESE AND OUT OF THIS WORLD APPS

The cosmos tell us all we need to know about ourselves. But can the stars also tell us what we like to eat? See if you're a match!

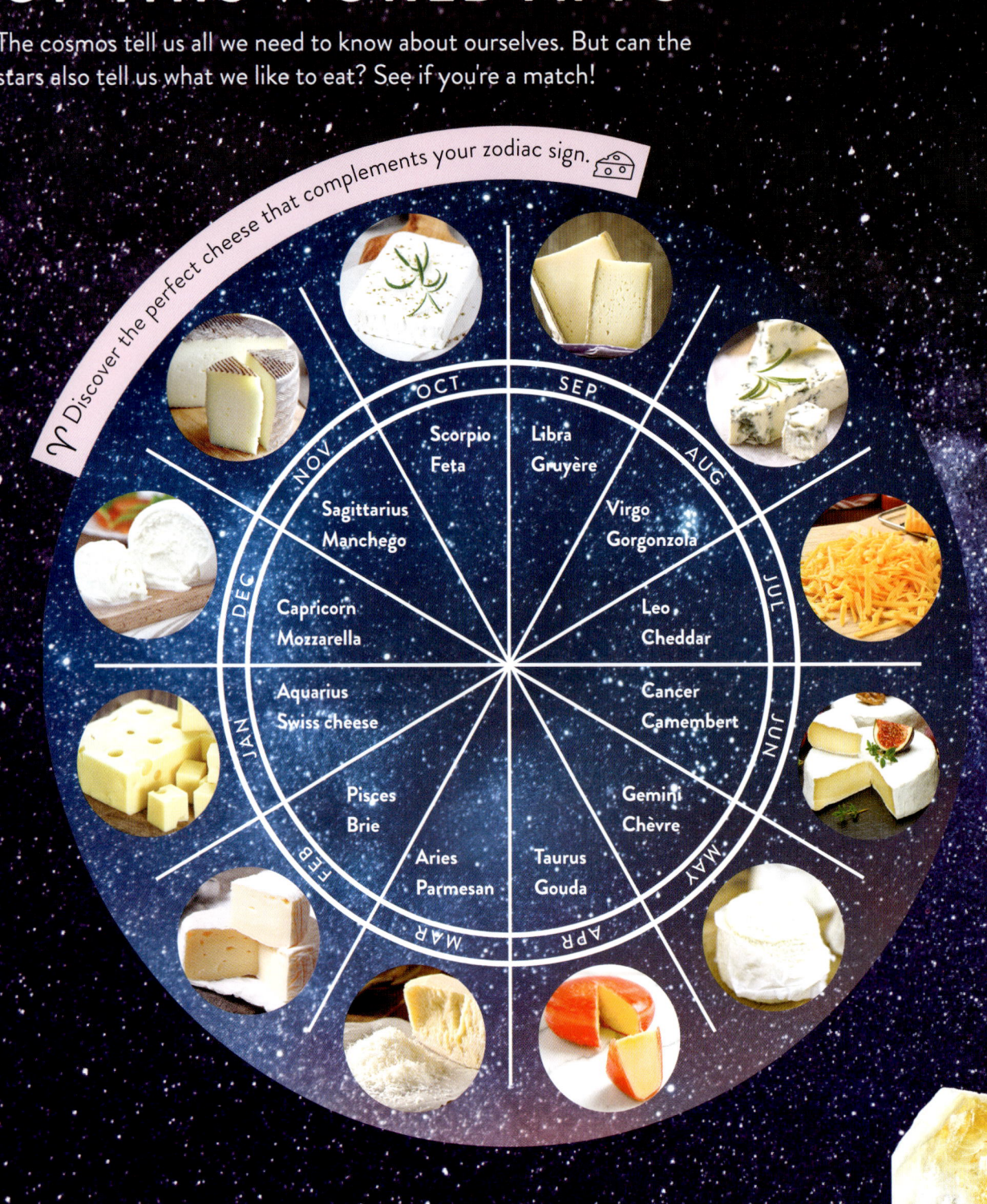

Discover the perfect cheese that complements your zodiac sign.

- Scorpio — Feta
- Libra — Gruyère
- Sagittarius — Manchego
- Virgo — Gorgonzola
- Capricorn — Mozzarella
- Leo — Cheddar
- Aquarius — Swiss cheese
- Cancer — Camembert
- Pisces — Brie
- Gemini — Chèvre
- Aries — Parmesan
- Taurus — Gouda

FOOD STYLING *Tips!*

"Purple cauliflower, olives, and roasted red pepper hummus will add just enough color for this cosmic theme spread. Take it the next level by smearing a dollop of hummus with a spoon to create a comet's tail!"

— Rosecleer

Watch the recipe video

SERVES 4

CHURRO CHOCO TACOS

I'm trying to understand the difference between wants and needs...
I want abs, but I NEED **churro** choco tacos!

INGREDIENTS:

1 tbsp jasmine rice

1 cinnamon stick

½ tbsp dry roasted almonds, chopped

1 cup heavy whipping cream, warm

¼ cup dulce de leche

1 cup melted butter

1 yellow cake mix pack

Cinnamon sugar

STEP 1

STEP 2

STEP 3

STEP 4

STEP 5

STEP 6

STEP 7

STEP 8

STEP 9

80

DIRECTIONS:

1. Place cinnamon stick, rice and ½ tsp almonds into an empty tea or mesh bag.

2. Place the packet into a bowl filled with the heavy whipping cream and let it infuse. Take the tea bag out of the whipping cream and let cool down.

3. Add ¼ cup of dulce de leche to the whipping cream and stir until mixed.

4. Whip the mixture using a high speed hand blender, pour into a loaf pan and drizzle dulce de leche on top. Grab a skewer and lightly swirl the dulce de leche into the mixture. Freeze for **3 hours** or until set.

5. In a large mixing bowl, stir together yellow cake mix and 1 cup of melted butter until combined.

6. Using a piping bag with an "open star" piping tip, pipe the churro batter onto parchment squares forming 3 inch round discs in the shape of a cookie.

7. Flip a muffin tin upside down and place the churro cookies between the pockets allowing them to bend and take on the shape of a taco shell. Freeze for **1 hour**.

8. Heat up vegetable oil to **350°F**. Drop the churro tacos into the oil and deep fry until golden brown.

9. Cover warm churro taco in cinnamon sugar. Scoop horchata ice cream into the center and finish with melted chocolate and crushed almonds.

NA-CHO AVERAGE TACO BAR CHECK LIST

Planning a taco bar for your next gathering is a fun, easy way to level up your fiesta for your guests!

TACO BAR Checklist

MEAT
- [ ] Seasoned Ground Beef
- [ ] Pork Carnitas
- [ ] Pulled Pork
- [ ] Shredded Pork

SHELLS
- [ ] Hard Sheels
- [ ] Soft Corn Shells
- [ ] Soft Flour Shells
- [ ] Tortilla Chips
- [ ] Tostadas

- [ ] **SHREDDED CHEESE**

SALSA OPTIONS
- [ ] Mild, Medium, Spicy
- [ ] Corn Salsa
- [ ] Pico De Gallo
- [ ] Salsa Verde

TACO TOPPING IDEAS
- [ ] Sour Cream
- [ ] Guacamole
- [ ] Onions
- [ ] Black Olives
- [ ] Cilantro
- [ ] Jarred Jalapeno Peppers
- [ ] Nacho Cheese

SIDE DISH IDEAS
- [ ] Black Beans
- [ ] Mexican Style Rice
- [ ] Plain Rice
- [ ] Refried Beans
- [ ] Cowboy Caviar
- [ ] 7 Layer Taco Dip
- [ ] Individual Bags of Fritos for "Walking Tacos"

FOOD STYLING *Tips!*

"Leave the avocado pit in your guac to keep it looking green and pretty for when your guests arrive. Add extra lemon or lime juice on top to help your guac stay bright and green!"

— Rosecleer

→ Use the two limes to hold up your shell while you fill it with yummy toppings

83

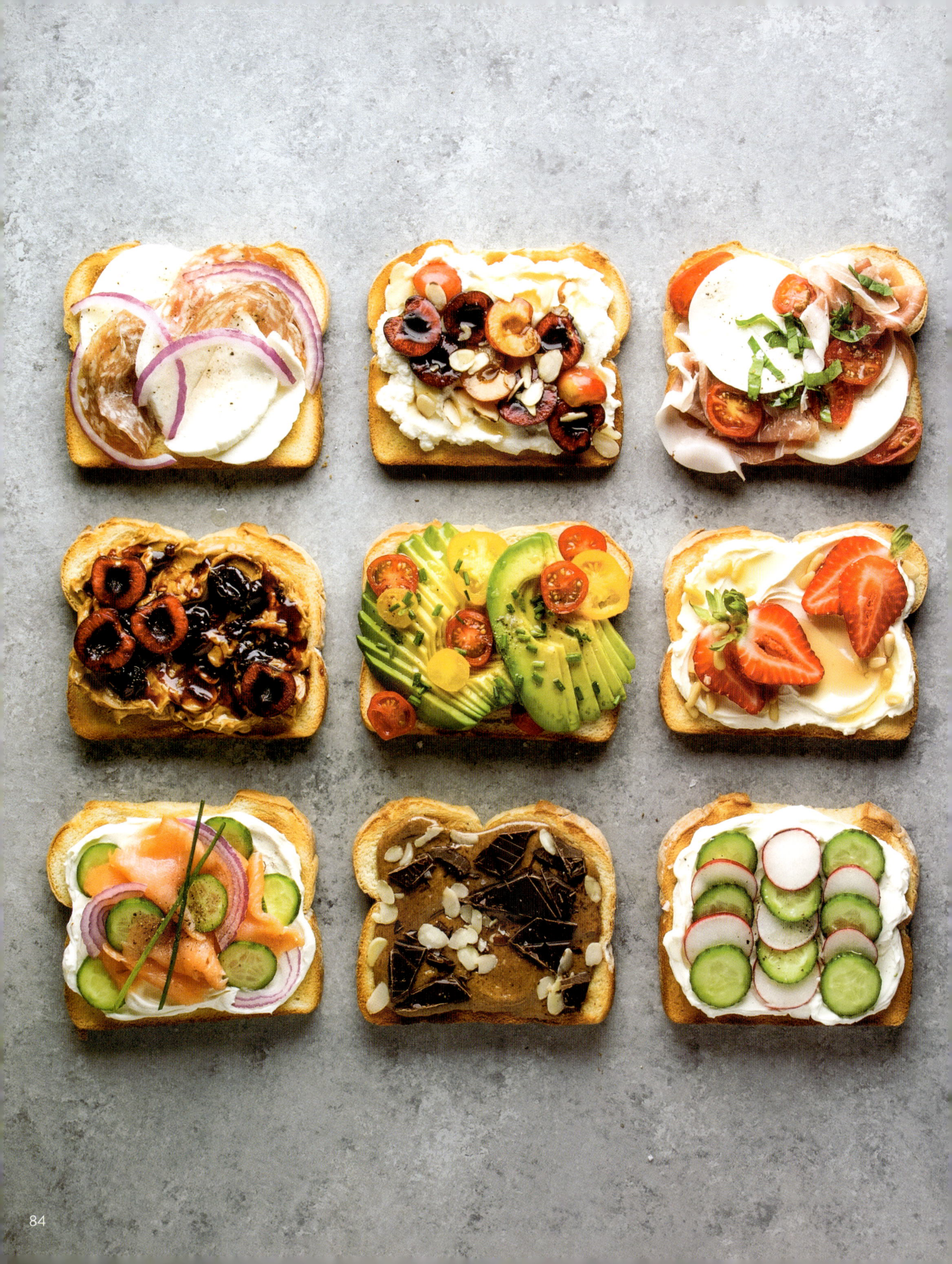

SERVES 1

UPGRADE YOUR TOAST GAME

Maximum flavor, minimal effort and Insta-worthy results! These toast ideas will make **mouths water** without breaking a sweat.

INGREDIENTS:

Simple Italian
Mozzarella
Salami
Red onion

Summer Cherry Jubilee
Almond
Cherry
Cream cheese
Honey

Caprese Supreme
Green Onion
Mozzarella
Salami
Tomato

Elvis Twist
Cherry
Jam butter
Peanut butter

The Avo
Avocado
Chives
Olive oil
Tomato

Strawberry and Cream
Cream cheese
Honey
Pine nuts
Strawberry

Lox Lover
Chive
Cream cheese
Cucumber
Salmon
Red onion

Sweet Tooth
Almond
Chocolate
Maple syrup
Peanut Butter

Cali Crunch
Cream Cheese
Cucumber
Radish

Lox Lover

Chive
Cream Cheese
Cucumber
Salmon
Red onion

Caprese Supreme

Green onion
Mozzarella
Salami
Tomato

VEGAN

The Avo

Avocado
Chives
Olive Oil
Tomato

+ Add salt & pepper to savory toast

Simple Italian

Mozzarella
Salami
Red onion

Cali Crunch

Cream Cheese
Cucumber
Radish

Summer Cherry Jubilee

Almond   Cream cheese
Cherry   Honey

Strawberries and Cream

Cream cheese   Pine nuts
Honey   Strawberry

Sweet Tooth

Almond   Maple syrup
Chocolate   Peanut Butter

Elvis Twist

Cherry
Jam butter
Peanut butter

Watch the recipe video

+ cooling time | 15

SERVES 5

INCREDIBLE EDIBLE BALLOONS

Your guests will be floating on air when they find out that you actually MADE these **edible balloons**!

INGREDIENTS:

Gummy bears (flavors of your choice)

Jolly Rancher gummies

"

With these (and any candy-based decorations), make sure to store your cake in a cool, dry place until you're ready to serve it. Too much time in the sun and these beautiful balloons can lose their lift!

— Mike

STEP 1

STEP 2

STEP 3

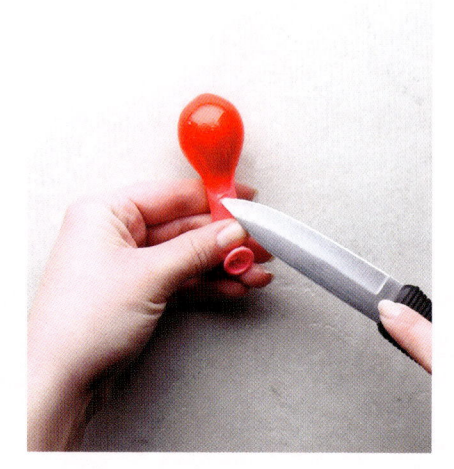

STEP 4

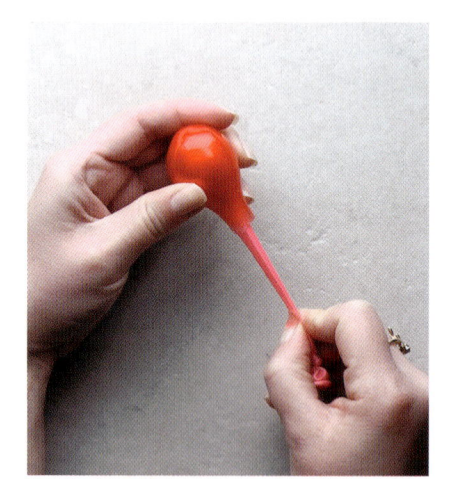

STEP 5

STEP 6

DIRECTIONS:

1. Melt the gummy bears in a double boiler. Stir until fully melted.
2. Dip partially inflated balloons in the melted gummy bears mixture. Refrigerate for **6 hours**.
3. Cut a small hole in the balloon.
4. Remove balloon from the shell.
5. Stick a gummy candy onto a paper straw and place the balloon onto the jolly rancher.
6. Decorate the top of the cake with the rest of the balloons.

Pretty Enough to Eat!

Edible flowers are the picture-perfect way to decorate your next dessert!

DANDELION

ROSE

NASTURTIUM

CHAMOMILE

PANSY

DAISY

LAVENDER

BORAGE BLOSSOM

SUNFLOWER

FOOD STYLING *Tips!*

Edible flowers can be found at your local floral shop, farmers' market, or specialty online retailers. When purchasing your edible flowers, timing is key. Make sure you purchase them just as you are ready to decorate to ensure peak freshness.

Watch the
recipe video

92

⏱ 5

SERVES 1

WEDDING CAKE GOALS

Skip the ceremony and get straight to the honeymoon! You'll totally fall in love with this disgustingly **adorable cake** decorating hack!

INGREDIENTS:

- Strawberry cake slice
- Fresh strawberries
- Fresh raspberries
- Edible flowers
- Whipped cream
- Strawberry fruit puree
- Squeeze bottle

STEP 1

STEP 2

STEP 3

STEP 4

DIRECTIONS:

1. Place a slice of strawberry layer cake on a round white plate.

2. Garnish the cake with strawberries, raspberries, edible flowers and whipped cream dollops.

3. Using a squeeze bottle, place small circles of strawberry puree along the edge of the plate starting from from large to small.

4. Run a skewer through the dots to connect them and create a romantic heart pattern!

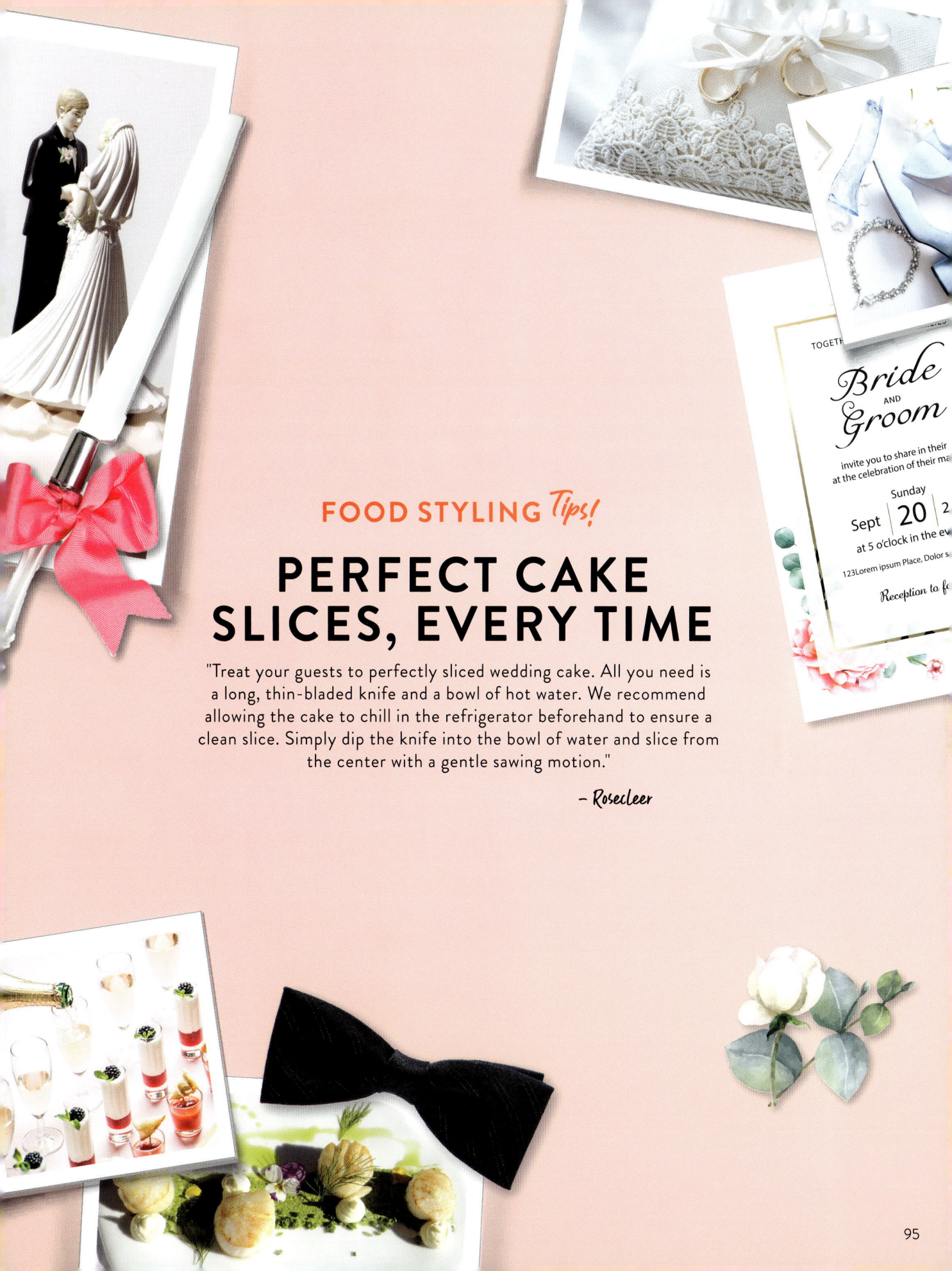

FOOD STYLING *Tips!*

PERFECT CAKE SLICES, EVERY TIME

"Treat your guests to perfectly sliced wedding cake. All you need is a long, thin-bladed knife and a bowl of hot water. We recommend allowing the cake to chill in the refrigerator beforehand to ensure a clean slice. Simply dip the knife into the bowl of water and slice from the center with a gentle sawing motion."

— *Rosecleer*

Watch the recipe video

60

16 CANDLES

EDIBLE BIRTHDAY CANDLES

Have your cake and eat your candles too! Nothing says "Happy Birthday" like these **eco-friendly edible candles** that will impress your friends while preserving the planet!

INGREDIENTS:

Mason jar

Smoothie straws

Candy melts

Sunflower seeds

"

The problem with wax candles is that they drip inedible wax all over your cakes! These edible versions can drip all they like, because they taste delicious!

— *Ira*

STEP 1

STEP 2

STEP 3

STEP 4

STEP 5

STEP 6

DIRECTIONS:

1. Melt the candy melts in a mason jar, placing several smoothie straws vertically into the melted mixture.

2. Let the mixture harden with the straws in it.

3. Remove the straws from the mixture and squeeze the hardened candy melt mixture out of them. This is the base of your candle.

4. Melt the top of the "candle" with a lighter and push the sunflower seed into the melted part, gluing it in place.

5. Repeat with different candy melt colors (optional).

6. Decorate your cake, light the seeds, and let the candles melt!

LET'S FACE IT, A NICE CREAMY CHOCOLATE CAKE DOES A LOT FOR A LOT OF PEOPLE; IT DOES FOR ME.

—Audrey Hepburn

Watch the recipe video

CHOCOLATE LACE CAGE CAKE

This impressive **cocoa creation** will have you wondering if you went to french pastry school in your past life.

INGREDIENTS:

Melted dark chocolate

> If you don't have a plastic bag to rip open, feel free to use parchment paper! Also, don't forget to let your chocolate cool (2 - 4 minutes) before you create your design.
>
> *– Miranda*

STEP 1

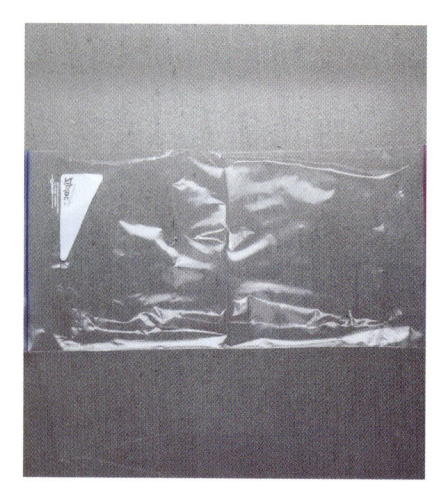

STEP 2

STEP 3

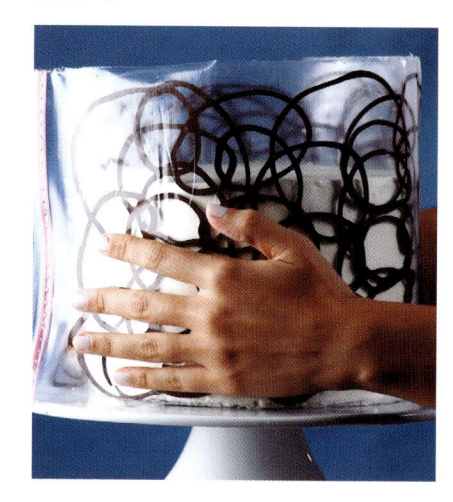

STEP 4

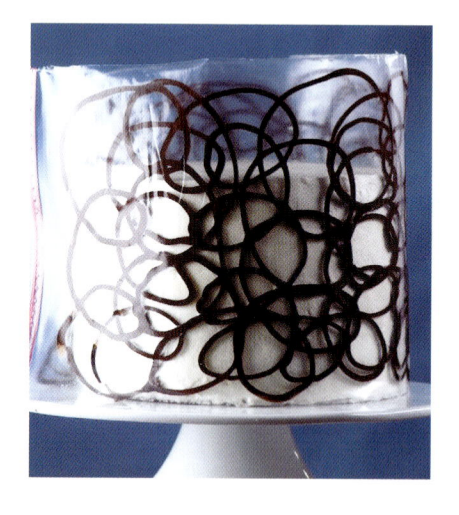

STEP 5

DIRECTIONS:

1. Add melted chocolate to a piping bag. Rip the seams on the side of a gallon-sized Ziploc bag and lay it flat.

2. Pipe the melted chocolate onto the open bag in a lacy swirl pattern.

3. Wrap the the Ziploc bag, chocolate side down around your cake.

4. Leave the bag on the cake until the chocolate is completely set.

5. Gently peel the collar off when the chocolate is hard.

10 TIPS TO THROW A PARTY ON A BUDGET

1.
Go veggie! With everyone trying to reduce their carbon footprint, take the meatless monday trend into the weekend by serving up tofu tacos or vegetarian nachos!

2.
Make it a potluck! Most people love an excuse to make that cheesy artichoke dip that they probably shouldn't eat alone in their apartment. Start a list of things people can bring and if they can't cook, **wine always works!**

3.
DIY your dessert! This chocolate cage cake is the perfect way to dress up a boxed cake that everyone thought was bought at a bakery.

4.
Hit up your local dollar store. Scope it out before you make up your theme so you can buy the majority of your party decor for a **fraction of the price.**

5.
Host an outdoor shindig. Most of the time, weather permitting, nature can provide more decor than your studio apartment. A few balloons and some twinkly lights go a long when when planning a **party on a budget**.

6.
Use an evite! There are so many great paperless invitation sites out there which make the planning process cheaper and easier for you! It's also way better for the environment!

7.
Host a game night! Have your friends bring their favorite games and vote on which game you will play as a group! Nostalgic games like pictionary and charades are great for a group and hilarious too!

8.
Make a signature cocktail. Rather than raid your freezer or spend a fortune, buy a decent selection of beer and soda and then make a signature cocktail using a less expensive liquor. Come up with a fun name and place it in a pitcher with fancy cups and straws.

9.
Use what you've got. Breakout that tea set you bought at the flea market last year and **have a tea party!** Pull out those moroccan scarves you got on that family vacation, put some pillows on the floor and have an Arabian Nights themed party. Get creative and your next gathering will be sure to stand out from the rest.

10.
Have a pancake and pajama party! There's nothing cheaper than a few packages of bacon and a box of pancake mix! Throw some fun pillows and blankets on the floor, serve mimosas and have the breakfast club on in the background. You have no idea how many people will be thrilled to trade in their stilettos for slippers!

Watch the recipe video

+ Baking time
50
SERVES 8

3-LAYERED STRAWBERRY FIELD CAKE

Damn, Gina! That cake is Gorge! Let's be honest, you might as well open up your own bakery after making this **amazing** cake!

INGREDIENTS:

2 ½ cups unsalted butter, softened

3 cups superfine sugar

9 large eggs

1 cup self-raising flour

3 ½ cups all purpose flour

3 tbsp whole milk

1 tsp vanilla extract

FILLING:

4 graham crackers, crushed

¼ cup unsalted butter, melted

¼ cup honey

⅓ cup strawberry jam

GARNISH:

1 lb strawberries, washed, and trimmed

SWISS MERINGUE BUTTERCREAM:

6 egg whites, room temp

1 cup granulated sugar

3 sticks unsalted butter, softened

2 tsp of vanilla

STEP 1

STEP 2

STEP 3

STEP 4

STEP 5

Check out how to make the perfect ombré cake on page 111

DIRECTIONS:

1. Trim the tops of the cakes to level them. Arrange whole strawberries trimmed side down onto the first cake layer. Use frosting to fill in the spaces around the strawberries, smooth with a spatula and gently add the next layer of cake.

2. Prepare your filling by mixing together graham cracker crumbs, butter, and honey. Spread this mixture onto the layer you just placed followed by another layer.

3. Spread jam over the top of the final layer.

4. Next, take your darkest shade of frosting and pipe two to three rings along the bottom of the cake. Then, take your medium shade and pipe two to three rings on top of that. Then, finish covering the rest of your cake, including the top, with your lightest color. Take a bench scraper or offset spatula and smooth the frostings down. Once the cake is smooth on the sides, move onto the top, and as soon as the cake is as smooth as can be, begin decorating. It is A-OK if the colors get a little mixed together as you go, that just adds to the ombre effect. If you want a SUPER clean stripe look, make sure you clean off your bench scraper or spatula every time you swipe the cake.

5. Decorate the cake with white chocolate covered strawberries!

EXCLUSIVE CONTENT!

All About Frosting

HOW TO
MAKE FROSTING IN 3 EASY STEPS

1. In a stand mixer with a paddle attachment on medium speed whip egg whites and granulated sugar, just until sugar is moist and well incorporated, then add vanilla.

2. Over a double boiler gently whisk egg mixture and beat on highest setting for about **8-9 minutes** until stiff peaks form.

3. Once the bowl cools down, slowly add softened butter until it becomes light in texture.

HOW TO
MAKE YOUR FROSTING SMOOTH

Ever wonder how to make your cake look as smooth as a baby's...well, you get what I mean! With just a few tools and some simple tricks, all of your friends will be begging you to bake for their next birthday!

Watch the recipe video

PURPLE OMBRÉ CAKE

SERVES 12

No matter how you slice it, your "hombres" are going to **LOVE** this ombre cake! It's like berry balayage in your mouth!

INGREDIENTS:

3 boxes lemon cake mix, prepared according to instructions

½ lemon

½ cup sugar

1 pint of blueberries

Swiss buttercream

3 tbsp blueberry jam

Purple food dye

Macarons

Mini meringues

Edible flowers, such as pansies or lavender

Fresh mint

STEP 1

STEP 2

STEP 3

STEP 4

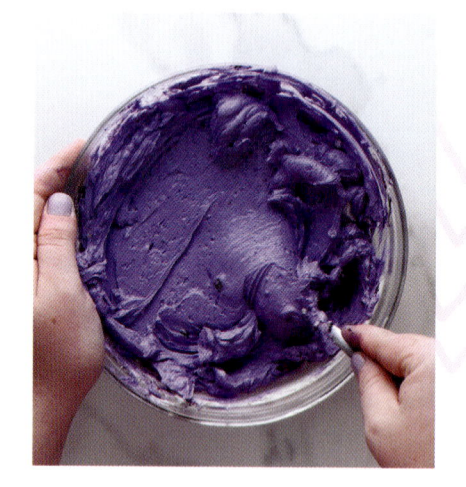

STEP 5

STEP 6

STEP 7

DIRECTIONS:

1. Starting with the cake, prepare the cake mix and split it evenly between three greased and lined, 9 inch cake pans.

2. Place a colander over an empty bowl. Place the blueberries in the colander. Then, squeeze the lemon half over the berries, and cover them with the sugar. Shake the colander until the berries are completely covered and crystalized looking.

3. Divide the sugared berries equally amongst the cake pans, and using a spatula, gently smooth the cake batter over them. We do this so the berries will intermittently polka dot the cake layers, if you're too rough with them they'll sink to the bottom and you'll have a delicious, but not super instagrammable, blueberry upside down cake. Once the blueberries are submerged (and it's okay if a couple are peeking out!) bake them according to box instructions.

4. Take your swiss buttercream and divide it into three bowls. To each bowl add 1 tbsp of blueberry jam. Once the jam is dispersed, add one drop of food coloring into the first bowl, two to the second bowl, and three to the third bowl. Mix them all up and spoon into individual piping bags.

5. Once the cakes are completely cooled and leveled, place a dollop of frosting onto a cake stand and place your first layer at the bottom. Place a thick layer of frosting on top, and this can be whichever one of the colors you like best! Spread, layer, spread, layer, you know the drill.

6. Next, take your darkest shade of frosting and pipe two to three rings along the bottom of the cake. Then, take your medium shade and pipe two to three rings on top of that. Then, finish covering the rest of your cake, including the top, with your lightest color.
Take a bench scraper or offset spatula and smooth the frostings down. Once the cake is smooth on the sides, move onto the top, and as soon as the cake is as smooth as can be, begin decorating. It is A-OK if the colors get a little mixed together as you go, that just adds to the ombré effect. If you want a SUPER clean stripe look, make sure you clean off your bench scraper or spatula every time you swipe the cake.

7. For our decoration, we created a crescent of decorations around the top of the cake. We used macarons, blueberry meringues, blueberries, mint leaves, lavender flowers, and purple pansies.

EXCLUSIVE CONTENT

HOW TO GET THE PERFECT OMBRÉ

Watch the recipe video

SERVES 8-10

CHECKERBOARD NEAPOLITAN CAKE

When you can't decide on chocolate, strawberry or vanilla, **just eat all three**!

INGREDIENTS:

Strawberry buttercream

Round vanilla cake

Round chocolate cake

Round strawberry cake

Chocolate ganache

"

Try experimenting with different ice cream/cake combinations! Two of my favorites are coffee frosting with yellow cake, and cookies 'n cream frosting with red velvet.

— Mike

STEP 1

STEP 2

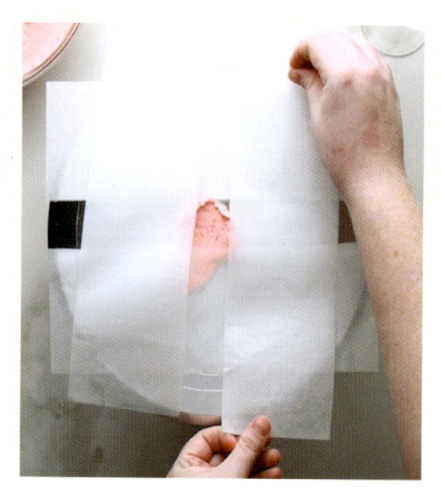

STEP 3

STEP 4

STEP 5

STEP 6

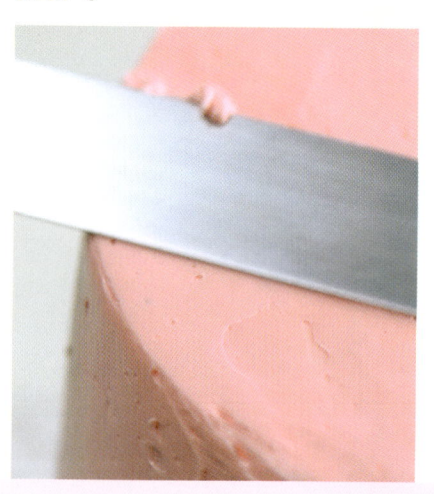

STEP 7

STEP 8

DIRECTIONS:

CHECKERBOARDING

1. Use a wine glass to cut the very middle circle. Repeat with all three cake. Cut the middle circle with a 5-inch bowl. Repeat.

2. Place a dollop of frosting in the middle of a cake stand. Place some parchment paper down and start stacking your cake rounds. For the first layer: chocolate center, vanilla middle, strawberry outside.

3. Very thin layer of frosting in between.

4. For the second layer, strawberry center, chocolate middle, vanilla outside. Frost.

5. For the third and final layer: vanilla center, strawberry middle, chocolate outside.

6. Frost and then frost the outside of the cake. GO THICK. If you are doing the chocolate swirl, a slightly thicker outer layer of frosting works better.

CHOCOLATE SWIRL (10 MINS)

7. Bring in some chocolate ganache in a squeezy bottle. Draw a snowflake on the top of the cake. Make sure the drips go down the side and do side drips in between the drips. Make sure your drips go all the way down.

8. Then, use an offset spatula or a butter knife, and spinning your cake stand, spin the knife around the sides of the cake and all the way onto the top. This will give your cake a swirled look.

DECORATING (10 MINS)

This cake is so swirly and exciting, so it is important that we keep the decorating to a MINIMUM, so pick one-quarter sliver of your cake (maybe one where you messed up the design! Garnishing is a great way to cover up any mistakes!). We decorated with a couple of strawberries, macarons, and white chocolate truffles, but you can use whatever you want.

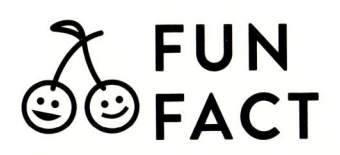

FUN FACT

Neapolitan ice cream was named in the late 19th century as a reflection of its presumed origins in the cuisine of the Italian city of Naples, and the many Neapolitan immigrants who brought their expertise in frozen desserts with them to the United States. Spumone, [a pistachio ice cream] was introduced to the United States in the 1870s as Neapolitan-style ice cream. Early recipes used a variety of flavors; however, the number of three molded together was a common denominator, to resemble the Italian flag.

Watch the recipe video

MAGICAL MONET CAKE

This cake is good from afar and even **better close up**! The only art degree you need for this cake is a sweet tooth!

INGREDIENTS:

Red and blue food coloring

2 tsps almond extract

Leftover baguette

> Once you've spread some of the food coloring on the frosting with your paper towel make sure to get a new one for every section of the cake, that way your colors stand out more!
>
> – Miranda

STEP 1 STEP 2  STEP 3

STEP 4  STEP 5

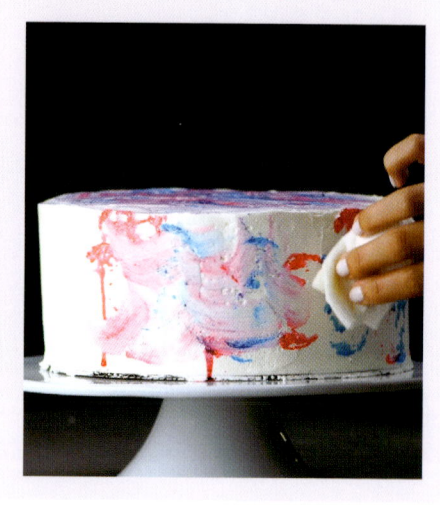

DIRECTIONS:

1. Place a few drops of food coloring and almond extract into a shallow dish.
2. Dip a piece of the baguette into the mixture until the dye has soaked the bread.
3. Stamp the dyed end of the baguette all over the cake.
4. Go back in with a second color using a new section of bread.
5. Use a slightly damp paper towel to brush over the cake and mix the colors.

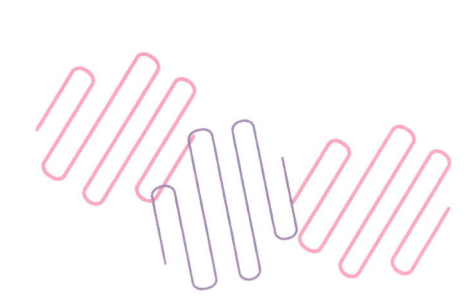

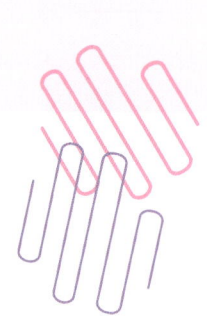

EXCLUSIVE CONTENT

KITCHEN ITEMS THAT CAN BE USED TO "STAMP"!

SPIRAL EGG BEATER

CELERY

WIRE MASHER

APPLE

CITRUS

POTATO

OKRA

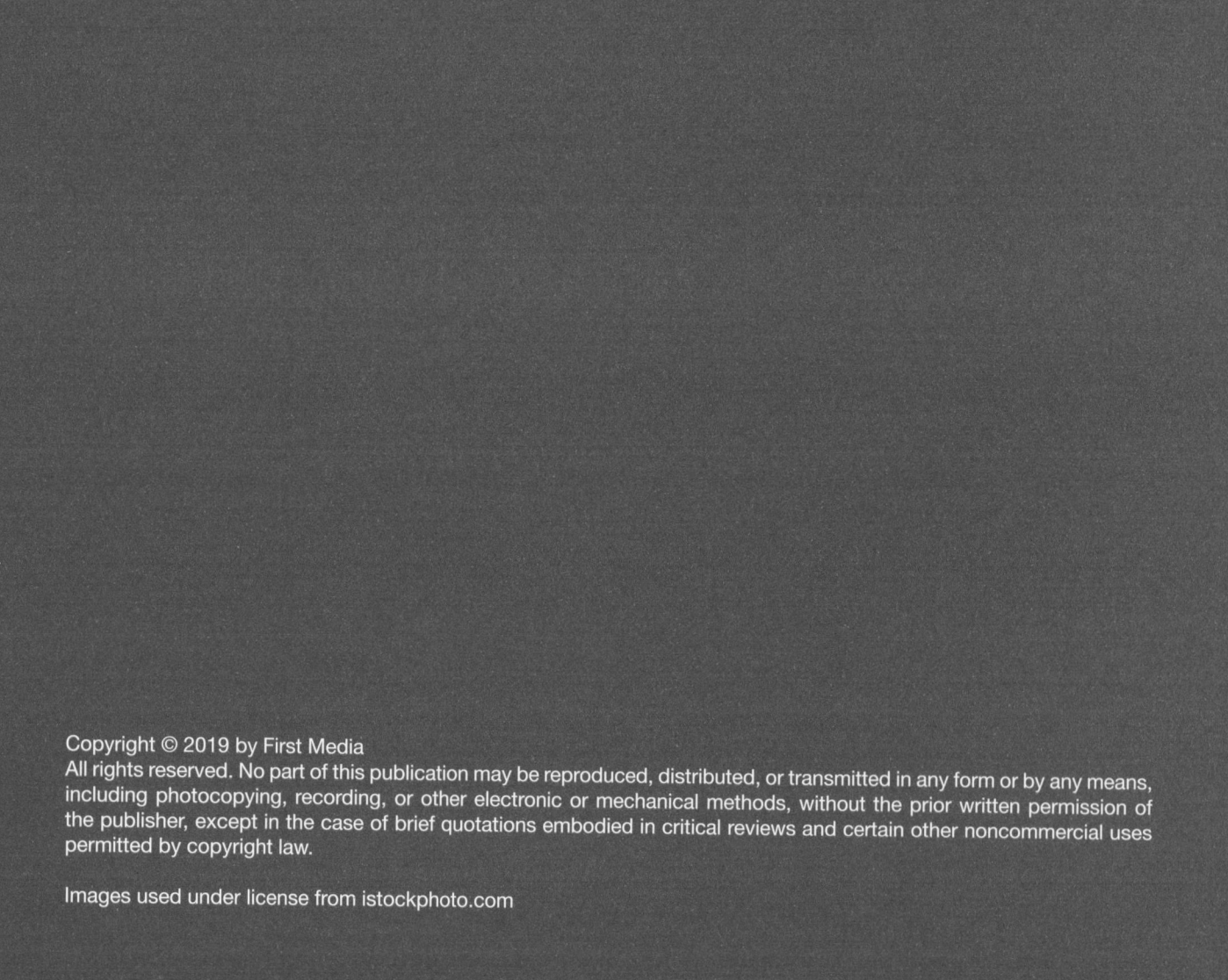

Copyright © 2019 by First Media
All rights reserved. No part of this publication may be reproduced, distributed, or transmitted in any form or by any means, including photocopying, recording, or other electronic or mechanical methods, without the prior written permission of the publisher, except in the case of brief quotations embodied in critical reviews and certain other noncommercial uses permitted by copyright law.

Images used under license from istockphoto.com